C000160499

Cornish Cheeses

Caryl Minson

Tor Mark · Redruth

The Cornish Tor Mark series

First published 2003 by
Tor Mark Press, PO Box 4, Redruth, Cornwall TR16 5YX
© 2003 Caryl Minson
ISBN 0-85025-400-0

The cover photograph is by Andrew Besley

Printed in Great Britain by R Booth (The Troutbeck Press)
Mabe, Penryn, Cornwall

What is Cheese?

Cheese is appetising, it is nutritious, and above all it is versatile.

Milk itself is a unique food. When infant mammals take their mother's milk, it is the only time that a single food provides for the whole of that animal's nutrition. For this reason, milk contains a very large range of nutrients.

Cheese, which is made from this valuable liquid food, shares many of the nutrients inherent in milk; but because we have separated the curds from the whey, there are differences in composition between the two foods.

Cheese is extremely rich in protein – a protein that is of particularly high quality. For most of us who possibly eat more than enough protein, this is not particularly important. But this high quality protein can be of real benefit to anyone suffering from certain severe or chronic illnesses.

Cereal protein is of lower quality than cheese protein, but cheese eaten with cereal products has the ability to enhance the value of the cereal protein. So the old established custom of eating bread and cheese together has a basis in scientific fact.

Hard cheeses contain little or no milk sugar (lactose), so sufferers from lactose intolerance may find that a small amount of this food added to their diet will not cause the problems associated with milk. Some soft cheeses do retain some of the whey and should therefore be eaten with caution.

The fat content differs widely between the different cheese types. Hard cheeses are rich in fat; cottage cheeses and similar types are low in fat content.

Cheese is the richest source of calcium of any common food. Although green vegetables are also a good calcium source, a greater proportion of this vital mineral can be utilised from cheese. As well as calcium, cheese also contains a wide variety of other essential minerals and vitamins.

It is now well known that eating cheese helps to protect teeth from decay. This is partly because cheese stimulates the flow of saliva, which is antibacterial in itself, but it also bathes the teeth in a rich mixture of minerals helping to preserve the enamel. So yet another custom is based on good scientific fact – ending a meal with a small piece of cheese.

Cheese Throughout the Centuries

For such an ancient, universal food, cheese makes very few appearances in literature, especially by comparison with wine. Cheese, like bread, was a staple of life, generally too common to mention. Shakespeare refers to 'toasted cheese' in *The Merry Wives of Windsor*, where it is snack food in a pub.

The great diarist, Samuel Pepys, gives us a much wider insight into its place in society, with twenty or more references in the *Diary*. First and foremost it was a convenience food – it did not require cooking. He ate bread and cheese as lunch or as a snack, sometimes while on horseback, and often just before bedtime.

But Pepys also provided cheese at the sumptuous dinners which, as he grew richer, he was proud of providing for his friends and acquaintances: 'I had for them, after oysters – at first course a hash of rabbits and lamb and a rare chine of beef – next a great dish of roasted fowl, cost me about 30s, and a tart; and then fruit and cheese. My dinner was noble and enough.'

Imported cheeses were not unknown. Pepys bought a couple of 'hollands cheeses' from a Dutch ship in the Thames, during a lull in the endless wars with the Dutch; and during the Great Fire of London, when panic-stricken householders were removing their valuables as the flames crept towards their houses, Pepys records this wonderful scene:

'Sir W Batten, not knowing how to remove his wine, did dig a pit in the garden and laid it in there; and I took the opportunity of laying all the papers of my office that I could not otherwise dispose of. And in the evening Sir W Penn and I did dig another and put our wine in it, and I my parmazan cheese as well as my wine and some other things.'

Pepys clearly valued his parmesan very highly! Sir William

Batten, incidentally, was to give his name to Mount Batten in Plymouth and Sir William Penn gave his to Pennsylvania.

Cheshire cheese was well thought-of but a Suffolk cheese, produced from the skimmed milk left after rich cream cheeses had been made for the gentry, was unlikely to feature at a banquet. In 1661 he records: 'So we stayed not to see [Webster's play *The White Devil*] but went out and drank a bottle or two of China-ale, and so I home – where I find my wife vexed at her people for grumbling to eat Suffolk cheese – which I am also vexed at.'

Pepys and his wife had only just become affluent enough to afford servants, a girl of seventeen and a foot-boy aged about ten, and it is quite possible they would have eaten Suffolk cheese themselves as an economy measure so it was galling to have the servants turning up their noses!

'Banbury Cheeses' was a nickname in general usage to describe those who were not living off the fat of the land and were therefore more than a little thin and scraggy themselves, and not full of the bonhomie that follows a good meal. Banbury was a notorious Puritan stronghold. Its cheeses were described as 'all rind' because they were hard, due to their depleted fat content.

All foods, whether berries, vegetables, fruit from trees, cereals and even the animals raised on the land, have always needed to be salted away, stored in cool larders, pickled in vinegar, or ground and stored in sacks. The ways and means of ensuring a year's supply of food, all harvested within a few short months, are centuries old. Such methods were identified long before freezers, dehydration and vacuum packing facilitated storage of perishable food.

Milk is no exception. Cheese has been made wherever an excess of milk production demanded, mostly in the Spring. The liquid food has to be stored in some longer term way. The first happy accident probably occurred in a family somewhere in Asia, who found, on return from a day's hunting and gathering, that the milk they had so providently put into the stomach bag of a newly killed kid had separated out. The harder bits of curd floating in the amber whey proved a welcome addition to their daily meals.

Milk 'goes off' within hours in a warm climate. The methods of making a more convenient food from it have evolved into many types of cheese, but the basic aim of storing milk as a solid remains the same. Adding a coagulating enzyme achieves what our stomachs do naturally, separating out the two parts – the curds from the whey – and preserving the more valuable curds in a far less perishable form.

That original family in Asia must have found the curd which remained after their meal had later hardened on the outside. Wondering if it was still of use to them, they would have broken open the lump to find that, inside, the white flesh of the cheese was sweet, nutty and very pleasant to eat.

We know that sheep and goats were domesticated as far back as 9000 years ago. As the herdsmen of these flocks moved around Asia, they would snap off any stick from a nearby plant to stir their souring milk. They found quite quickly that a stem from a fig tree, or certain local herbs, helped the lumps of curd stick together and become a mass, which could be handled easily.

Age-old rock drawings of dairying have been found in the Libyan desert. A clay pot in an Egyptian tomb contained a piece of cheese. Obvious sustenance for the hereafter!

Cheese is mentioned throughout the Bible, but the Greeks were sure that this divine food had come as a gift from their own gods. Aristotle compared the transforming of the liquid milk into the solid cheese to the beginning of human life. Fig branches were used during this period as a coagulant, the Romans using this and many other plant forms to create their hard cheeses. As the Roman armies advanced over Europe and into Britain, it was cheese which nourished them on the way and cheese-making was quickly taught to the conquered races, making sure that this food would be easily available.

Oils from dairy products have been found in British pottery 6000 years old; soft cheeses had been made here in Britain long before the arrival of the Romans: but with their more advanced knowledge of a coagulant being applied to the curds, the whey being pressed out, and the resulting mass salted and left to dry in the sun, cheese-making took a major step forward. The Romans also taught the Britons how to make different cheeses. They brined some, smoked others and coloured some with saffron.

During the dark ages, this expertise was held in the monasteries. Cheese was an important food, since meat was forbidden on so many fast days. The variety of cheeses that they could produce must certainly have been a blessing in their otherwise basic diet.

Cows began to take over from sheep and goats as the major milk animal during the Middle Ages. The greater volume of milk was an important factor, although goat's and ewe's milk was still appreciated to make the finer cheeses.

'Hard cheese' perhaps began at this time to be an expression of sympathy as well as a description for the quality of the cheese made from the skimmed milk after the richer cream cheeses had gone upstairs. Rock hard and dry, these lower order cheeses could be relied on to last through a hard winter, and to make the midday meal for the workers on the estate.

Cream cheeses and simple fresh curd cheeses were known as 'green' cheeses, indicating the quality of their freshness in the same way as with 'green' wine; it did not imply they were coloured green. After the curds had been formed into a shape, they were laid on woven mats covered with nettle leaves to act as an aid to drainage and to repel the flies with the antiseptic aroma of the nettles. In many places around Britain these 'green' cheeses were referred to as nettle cheeses, but the nettles did not act as a rind as they do with the modern Cornish Yarg.

Methods of making particular cheeses were passed down through families, often from mother to daughter. Many famous women 'invented' some of the well-known names that we enjoy today. However nobody really invents or makes a cheese that has not been made before. In the same way, all cooking is a slant on something that someone else has made centuries before, or in another country. The differing conditions with which a cheese-maker has to contend all help to style a cheese, even if it is based on an original of many thousands of years ago. The knowledge is passed down, but it is the craftsmanship which enables a cheese-maker to produce a consistent cheese which customers can instantly recognise and name.

Cheeses were made with unpasteurised milk until the middle of the nineteenth century when Louis Pasteur changed the style of cheeses for all time, by bringing pasteurisation to the world. This made large scale cheese production possible, which had a good side in meeting the increasing world need for food; but at the same time it reduced the range of individual cheeses.

We are indeed lucky in Cornwall. There is a very large range of individual cheeses made here, both pasteurised and unpasteurised – all of them drawing on the expertise and experience of a millennium and more years. Choice is available, and pleasure at the table undoubted.

Windows in the Dairy

'Wherever there is a farm, there will be a dairy in the farmhouse.' Sadly that law does not apply in this century. There are now enormous farms scattered around the countryside of England. The product of these farms, never, never makes its way into the farm kitchen. It is boxed, then palleted, to make a long journey into a packing centre; there it is further processed into the small packages of ready-to-eat vegetables, dairy produce or meat that we like to find on our supermarket shelves.

In the nineteenth century, the dairy was still an important area of the farmhouse. Placed at the north end, where the house walls would be at their coolest, its floors and shelving were heavy slates.

Windows were a distinctive part of the dairy – latticed windows with shutters. Sadly, these had long gone when in the late 1980s I first came to Menallack Farm, near Penryn, but I was delighted to find a perfect example at a nearby farm which had so far escaped the renovation which also damages tradition. Delicate fan-shaped laths covered the window aperture. No paned glass was there, but internal shutters were just visible on the inside.

At the beginning of the nineteenth century, when other buildings were taxed on the number of windows they displayed, these working windows were considered so important that they were excluded from taxation, provided that they were clearly labelled for any inspection with a sign above the window saying 'Dairy' or 'Cheese Room'. I am indebted to Michael Cooper for this information and am delighted to add another piece to the jigsaw of knowledge about our old cheese craft.

As I have said, when we came to Menallack it had already been 'improved' by a total reconstruction. There was very little visible of the ancient granite dwelling that had served its many owners well for so many centuries. But there was one small original window on the north side of the farmhouse which did still have old shutters on the inside. With the deep window shelf sitting on the bulk of the thick granite wall, I found it an ideal place to mature my early 'Menallacks' while I was still making them in the farmhouse kitchen. Little did I realise that I was following in the path of previous cheese or clouted cream makers!

Some time ago we were doing a little renovation of our own, in this case demolishing some of the 1950s work in order to expose once again the lovely granite walls and charming wide-planked and beamed ceilings. We found, tucked up inside one of the plaster-boarded spaces, a small chamfered sign-board, professionally painted, bearing the word DAREY. We were thrilled to find it and amused, in our ignorance, at the spelling. But the word now has a deeper, more interesting explanation.

Work on the farms was divided. Field work was largely undertaken by the men, along with the care of the stock. Milking, churning and cheese-making was work for the women. A seventeenth century diary noted that a country woman needed 'a cool hand for butter, but a strong arm for cheese.' My present team would agree with this after an hour-long scalding and stirring of the curd!

In the Middle Ages, the word for a woman farm-servant was *dey*. The room where they worked, producing food from the milks of the various animals was (variously spelled) the *deyery*, and the work itself took on the same name.

It was an exciting discovery to realise that our small piece of wood, with its phonetic spelling, did indeed show that Menallack had some time before our arrival possessed a dairy window. Menallack, we felt, had revealed herself to be a lot older than we had perhaps realised.

The Unique Character of Regional Cheeses

'Any use, Mum?' said my one-syllabled conversation piece of a son, standing at the kitchen door, mindful of muddy boots, kitchen floors and irate mums. He jerked his head, indicating the bucket of milk he carried in his large left hand.

'Yes, put it there,' I replied, with my head and attention deeply inside a brewing pan on the Aga.

Some time later I gave the bucket, still frothy surfaced, my whole attention. Picking out the right book from my well stocked library, I thumbed through pages; it is the word salt which catches my eyes and stops my fingers on 'Cheshire cheese'.

One of England's oldest named cheeses, its character arises from the salty deposits lying under the grasses of that county. It touches a chord with me. Even though we are three miles inland, we have salt all around us, and a granite rock base for our patchwork meadows.

'Prime grass growing,' so my neighbour assured me when we moved in. And it is this grass that lies at the heart of most of Cornwall's agriculture.

In the 1540s, John Leland found that the best land was around the coast and was steadily being enclosed into small partitions of land, dressed and sanded to make it very fertile.

In the late sixteenth century, John Norden, making a survey of the county, considered that, though there was sufficient food to feed the populace, nevertheless the soil was poor, particularly in the middle part, 'being very moorish and craggie'.

Long before the Tudor period the landscape of west Cornwall as we know it today had begun to take shape. Each small area of land had been surrounded with the granite boulders that had worked their way up through the soil over millions of years. The first layer of stone was placed well below the surface of the soil, conserving the fall of rain to the soil lying inside the field. With the light loamy soil so characteristic of the coastal area of Cornwall, this was a stroke of genius to enrich the soil in the most natural way possible.

Farmers slowly enclosed yet another patch of moorland ground for arable farming and enriched the soil as best they could. Richard Carew in 1602 describes them removing turves, burning them, and mixing the ash with sea-sand, brought with great effort on packhorses from the nearest beach.

With very few trees in the county four hundred years ago, I would hate to imagine the quality and erosion of soil that would have happened without the enchanting small patchwork fields that we see most clearly when we are flying over Cornwall on our way to the Isles of Scilly.

Our green patchwork fields, edged with quaint hawthorn boundaries shaped by the wind, owe much of their charm to the grass which has been nurtured for centuries inside those four walls of granite strength.

Cornish grass becomes Cornish milk and, with a bow to our clouted cream, butter and ice-cream colleagues, expresses itself very well in Cornish cheese.

The Cornish Cheeses

We now have an abundance of cheeses. For a county which three hundred years ago drew forth a sour comment from one traveller that 'there were not many cheeses to be found in the whole of that county and what there was, was very bad!', we can now justifiably feel proud of the variety and richness of this harvest from our green patchworked fields.

Patrick Rance, who was always very supportive of Menallack cheeses, recalled in *The Great British Cheese Book* that in the 1940s the prevalent milking cow in Cornwall was the Guernsey. One of my working colleagues at Menallack, herself a farmer's wife, agrees with this and says that most of the farms around the Helford area were using Guernsey cows at that time. Their rich creamy milk naturally led to the famous 'clouted' cream of Cornwall. But even with such a delicious product as this, there can still be a surplus.

The cream was drained in muslin on a flat surface under a weight, after an initial drying off period, before being drained into muslin-lined moulds. These were individual oblong moulds: I would dearly love to know whether these were made of wood. I can imagine how simply creamy that little cheese was – and being only 4oz in weight, the indulgence would not have been too severe!

There are four broad classes of Cornish cheese. The greatest number use cow's milk, but a noticeable group have emerged over the past ten years using goat's milk, sheep's milk and most recently buffalo. Many restaurants use this range for their cheese course and visitors leave with a vivid memory of gastronomic pleasure – and hopefully some further supplies to take home!

Of the many types of cheeses now produced here in Cornwall, the largest section are still the hard and semi-hard cow's milk, followed by white-rinded, smoked, fresh soft and a blue semi-hard – quite enough choice to mount a magnificent cheeseboard. It would be hard to make a decision if one was forced to limit the board to four or five.

We are indeed lucky to have this superb range of a primary food, a food that can suit every person in the land from the newest of the newborn, to the oldest amongst us.

I remember vividly a proud new father reaching behind his shoulders to his young son to offer him a small piece of Cornish cheese. The contented sucking of this baby on the milky food was proof enough that cheese can sustain life from the very beginning right through to the point at which we turn full circle and again want an easy digestible protein to sustain us at the fullest of our age. I am regularly asked to prescribe an attractive small range of Cornish cheeses for 'my Great Uncle George, who lives on his own'.

With every new year the list is getting more exciting. There are certainly over thirty kinds, and if subtle variations on these are included the count could be nearer sixty. What new cheeses will future years bring to this moist green land stretching out into the sea?

Cornish Cheeses Today

Here is a list of cheeses present in the county today. There are other cheeses, which have fallen away; there will certainly be more to come – probably even before this book is published; but this is as up to date as we can go at the moment.

Hard and semi-hard cheeses made from cows milk

Davidstow
Cornish Yarg
Menallack Farmhouse
Vintage Menallack
St Laudus
Menallack Chives
Cornish Garland
Tiskey Meadow
Trelawny
Miss Muffet
Garden of Eden
Ambervale
Cornish Organic Cheddar
Wild Garlic Yarg
Stithians Special Keltic Gold

Davidstow is an award winning creamery cheddar made just outside Camelford. It draws milk from the surrounding farms of North Cornwall. Big though this factory is nowadays, it nevertheless started off as a farm based cooperative operation which has succeeded beyond the dreams of those first farmers eighty years ago.

This cheddar is superb used in any of the more conventional dishes using cheese, but do try it with fresh broccoli. There are also some wonderful pasties using this cheese with chopped onion, as well as splendid picnic pies using local bacon and apples with scattered nuggets of Davidstow cheddar. West Country pie with a difference!

Cornish Yarg was brought into Lynher Dairies just outside Liskeard by a young couple called Gray. (G-R-A-Y reversed spells Y-A-R-G!) Michael and Margaret Horrell continued expanding this centuries-old link of nettles with cheese, to produce a delicate nettle-rinded, handmade cheese which gives a fresh lemony flavour, softening and deepening with age. This pasteurised cheese combines with our local scallops as well as being ideal for soufflés or flans. It behaves impeccably as a melted cheese topping over a savoury vegetable dish.

In recent years Lynher Dairies has expanded into a partnership with Ben and Catherine Mead of Pengreep. Production of Cornish Yarg has begun there in a purpose-built creamery using the milk from the Pengreep herd of Friesians.

Cornish Wild Garlic Yarg, an innovation from Lynher Dairies, brilliantly uses the white flowered wild garlic that covers all our hedgerows in Spring, vying with the bluebells and other Spring flowers for an explosion of colour at that time. The strappy leaves are dealt with in the same way as the nettle, painted onto the fresh curd exterior. The cheese benefits enormously from the unmistakeable aroma of this garlicky plant, permeating the entire *pâte* (*pâte* is a French word for everything which is inside the rind or crust of the cheese).

Following the sad departure in Devon of the Peverstone Company making traditional cheeses (Devon Garland and Tiskey Meadow) the Lynher Partnership has brought these two excellent cheeses into their own group, re-christening the Garland to suit its new county and producing both with the same fresh semi-hard style as the well-known Yarg.

Cornish Garland using cows milk has an inner band of chopped spring onions and herbs.

Tiskey Meadow, uses chopped sun-dried tomatoes with herbs. Both cheeses are unrinded and pasteurised.

Menallack Farmhouse is a handmade cheese using the milk of only one herd. We follow a Cheshire style of making this unpasteurised cheese. It is matured on wooden shelves to achieve a rich distinctive taste and a natural rind, very reminiscent of the natural colours to be found in the granite of Cornwall.

This farmhouse cheese has the necessary strength to stand up to cider, beer or wine in a variety of robust cheese dishes and links well with meat or fish.

Vintage Menallack takes pride of place on a cheeseboard. There is no particular virtue using this larger wheel with its long taste in the kitchen, when there is a farmhouse Menallack available.

Trelawny, another farmhouse cheese, is made by Sue Proudfoot using the milk from the farm's herd of Friesians based just outside Bude at the top of the county. With a rich taste, creamy interior and a natural mould-ripened rind, this cheese has become deservedly popular with the general public. Ring the changes on the cheeseboard with Trelawny or consider it in a classic fondue with its sister, **Miss Muffet**.

Both cheeses are pasteurised, natural rinded and handmade; but Miss Muffet has the distinction over her brother Trelawny of being washed. Any gender distinction stops right there!

The name 'Miss Muffet' gives a hint as to the method of production. Once the curds have been separated from the whey, they are washed very thoroughly with water in almost a continental style and then salted, milled and placed into moulds. With the removal of any residual whey, a completely different taste is achieved making this newcomer to the Cornish front very distinctive.

Cornish Organic Cheddar is another fairly new arrival. In the nineties, John Gaylard took over the building once known as Old Lobbs Dairy. This spanking new creamery, set on the dramatic cliff tops of the north coast, is making this full flavoured black wax-coated cheese from Cornish organic milk.

Keltic Gold, the latest cheese from Whalesborough Farm, is thoroughly continental in character. The full round flavour of this pasteurised washed rind cheese deepens as it matures to a very pronounced and aromatic taste. The *pâte* is quite soft and sticky; the rind has an orange sheen.

Garden of Eden from Cornish Farmhouse Cheeses at Menallack uses sun-dried tomatoes well mixed in with the curds at the time of milling, to make a pleasantly moist cheese brimming with flavour after six weeks of maturing.

St Laudus is another truckle from Menallack Farm. Rodded with a blue culture at a very early stage, St Laudus is foil-wrapped to intensify the culture allowing it to permeate throughout the *pâte* inside the cheese. For all those who like a cheese with a very positive note, this is one to enjoy on the cheeseboard.

Menallack Chives follows a popular route, adding chopped chives and garlic at curd-milling time and using minimal maturing time to allow the freshness of the herbs to show at their best. This is an ideal cheese to cube into a pasta dish.

Ambervale, one of the first cheeses from the new Cornish Country Larder at Trevarrian, pleases many of our younger customers by the pleasant unalarming taste and texture; it is a cheerfully coloured waxed cheese. It appeals enormously to children returning from school in the afternoon. Ambervale will perform nicely straight on to a roll or more enterprisingly set to melt in the microwave to provide a quick snack.

Hard Cheeses using Goat's and Ewe's Milk

Tala

Polmesk

Village Green

Tala, a ewe's milk cheese, was produced outside Launceston by Heather and Hans White. Using the qualities of ewe's milk, well known for the smaller globules of protein, this washed-rind barrel-shaped cheese cuts into a very firm dense rind to reveal a distinctive and sophisticated *pâte*. It is now made at Menallack.

Like Village Green, Tala saves our lives when we have a guest to supper who is allergic to cow's milk. Ewe's milk being expensive to produce, litre for litre, it is economically wise to restrict use in the kitchen – save the pleasure for the cheeseboard. Many lovers of this cheese can relate it to the best of the Spanish manchego cheeses. Like ourselves, and many others in this hand crafted work, Hans and Heather came to cheese production from a widely differing lifestyle. Cheese making seems to attract a very varied range of people into its craft.

One of the best known examples of a change of lifestyle is, of course Leon Downey of Llangollen in Wales. Deciding to opt out of a prestigious career as a cellist, his second career as a talented cheesemaker has won him the same plaudits that he had achieved in the music world.

My own husband, who has taken over the technical running of the cheeseroom here at Menallack, was in his previous life travelling the world as a telecommunication engineer and manager. Getting the milk into vats at 6am on a chilly Spring morning is one more example of a total change of life style, to say nothing of temperature!

Polmesk, made at Menallack from the goat's milk of Polmesk Farm on the Roseland, started life – as many of the best cheeses have, and certainly the first historic one – by accident. The curds left in the colanders at the end of the cheesemaking day achieved an attractive ball shape when reversed into another colander. They were left to mature and dry in position, then brined and lightly waxed to keep the moistness in the cheese; we found that we had arrived at a cheese which was not soft, but was certainly not hard either. Our outlets liked it and the customers soon came back with a hefty vote for more.

Village Green, the notable goat cheddar, is made by John Gaylard of Cornish Country Larder. He came to the Lobbs Dairy at Trevarrian after a lifetime's experience dealing with goats and their cheeses at Cricket St Thomas. Setting up a completely new plant in this dramatic part of Cornwall was his dream and Village Green was the first of many cheeses to come from this modern creamery. Matured goat cheeses can suffer from the very quality which makes this milk so distinctive: the even and small distribution of protein makes a very dense texture, which can harden into dryness if a natural rind is chosen. Village Green is protected by a wax coat, allowing it to maintain moistness into full maturity.

White-rinded cheeses

St Endellion
Cornish Organic brie
St Mawgan (no longer available)
St Antony
Chatel
Gevrik
St Keverne Square
Toppenrose Gold

St Endellion. John Gaylard of Cornish Country Larder took the county by storm a few years ago, and won the gratitude of restaurants and hotels, with this, the first brie that he produced. St Endellion is a triple cream 900 gram brie and ripens to a delightful depth of taste.

Cornish Organic Brie soon followed. Noticeably different from the St Endellion, with the clean bright taste of the organic milk, it also has the benefit for many restaurants of having the choice of a bigger wheel nearer in size to the classic French brie. For the smaller domestic scene there is a 900 gram version as well.

Both bries are ideal choices for a cheeseboard when brought to properly glooping ripeness; I also enjoy playing with them in the kitchen, but then I have been cooking with all cheeses throughout my life – since, as a child I would put a slice of cheese in a frying pan at our Victorian house above Readymoney Cove in Fowey, when I knew that my mother was out for the afternoon. I can still remember that frying, burning smell!

You can have great fun with the classic deep fried recipes, remembering always to keep the cheese thoroughly chilled and using an immature brie or Fingal for your play. Do practice before the night! This is not a starter to make a dramatic entrance without previous rehearsal.

St Mawgan also followed, made from cow's milk and taking a cylindrical shape – appreciated by chefs for portion sizing. Sadly this cheese has now lapsed and is still mourned by some with long memories.

St Antony, using goat's milk, is an oblong 6 inch. Having the fine elastic *pâte* usual with a soft goat cheese, St Antony is excellent for grilling but also matures to a very acceptable cheese board piquance.

Chatel – Cornish for cattle – like St Endellion contains a portion of double cream. Again, an ideal picnic extra, as well as offering some exciting ideas to play with in the kitchen. This is one of two new cheeseboard contenders recently produced by Cornish Country Larder, the other being Gevrik.

Gevrik – Cornish for little goat – is a useful 70 gram cheese, with its sturdy packing ideal for picnics as well as enterprising use in the kitchen.

St Keverne Square is a white-rinded cheese using pasteurised milk and vegetarian renneted, made at Toppenrose Dairy by Mr and Mrs David Lambrick with their son Ben. They are another prime example of farmers who have diversified, using the advantages of their own farm out on the magical peninsula of the Lizard.

Toppenrose Gold is a small round cheese in which the Lambricks use their own pasteurised milk and the cream from a nearby farm. Both this and St Keverne Square are excellent in the picnic basket as well as deserving a place on the Cornish cheeseboard.

Smoked cheeses

Old Smokey
Cornish smoke
Tresco
Tintagel
Tesein

Olde Smokey uses the basic pasteurised Ambervale and is smoked with three fruit woods. This cheese is a pliable pleasantly tasted 7 inch round, about 1 inch in depth.

Cornish Smoke uses fourteen-month matured Davidstow cheddar which is then smoked with ash wood, making a fragrant addition to the alternatives on the cheese board.

Tresco, Tintagel and **Tresein** are all smoked by Nigel Ekins using the three fruit woods as with Ambervale. All three have won awards. This selection offers more variety on the cheeseboard for smoked cheese aficionados.

Blue cheeses

Cornish Blue

As I write, we have only one blue in Cornwall. This state of affairs I am sure will change as the years go on. We have proved in the last ten years that Cornwall is second to none in producing a variety and richness of cheeses from the grass fields and mild climate of our county.

Cornish Blue can, enviably from the marketing point of view, claim to come from Cheesewring Farm. Developed only recently, and introduced at the 2001 Royal Cornwall Show, it was universally acclaimed as 'not bad, you!' by the thousands who came past our stall there. Made on this moor farm high above Liskeard by Philip Stanfield, it follows a Gorgonzola production method and in the first months was charmingly misshapen – looking not unlike an elephant's foot. All cheeses evolve a little as they grow up and Cornish Blue is already changing to a more routine shape.

I am sure that its solitary status will change in the future, but for the present we can enjoy this soft, creamy rodded cheese principally on the cheeseboard. It will marry very well with a ripe William pear and finely-chopped celery for a starter. It will also blend with the flesh of an avocado and a small amount of finely chopped onion to make a tangy dip with crisp wafers or oatmeal biscuits.

Fresh Soft Cheeses

Vithen

Fingals

Cornish Feta

Cornish Pepper

Cornish Garlic and Herbs

Cornish Tarragon

Cousin Herbert

Buffalo Soft

Nanterrow

The fresh soft cheeses of Cornwall are increasing in variety by leaps and bounds. Some have gone, but others have taken their place; yet more will arrive in future, for this is the nature of these 'make today, eat tomorrow' little marvels. When I arrived back in the county at the end of the '80s there was a delightful cheese being made at St Columb by June Gurd, from the milk of her own goat herd. Called Vashti, it was a wonderful fresh trembling little cheese – but sadly no more. Vithen is a replacement for it.

In past centuries soft fresh cheeses would, like other farm produce, have been seasonal. A flush of Spring milk brings about not only the cheeses to set aside and mature, but also a fresh round half-pounder for this week's market.

It hardly needs saying, but I will: it is the character of fresh cheeses to be just that – *fresh*! From this two things follow. The essence of the taste will be freshness, not strength. Occasionally customers approach fresh cheeses with a cheddar expectancy in their taste buds. The second point is that if it is to stay fresh, your little cheese should not have travelled many miles before coming to your plate. We have invented some very sophisticated wrappings in the last century, so that cheeses can go out and about; but I can assure you that with every hour from their making these fresh cheeses are losing the very quality that is their charm. Find a local cheesemaker, ask when their soft cheese is being made that week, and grab it quick. It will be a fresh joy to your meal that very evening – and for that day only. Don't worry about placing it in the fridge. The colder temperature firms up the soft, almost tremulous, character of the curd – and another part of the delight will have gone. I do appreciate, however, that for a fresh cheese to be sold from a shop, then refrigerated it has to be.

Vithen, from Menallack, is one of those useful simple pasteurised cheeses which blends and mixes when a recipe says, 'Take 4 oz fresh goat's cheese'. But many Vithen afficionados appreciate it for the simplicity of its taste spread on a cracker or rye bread.

Fingals is one step up from Vithen. One of our first cheese-makers at Menallack was a five-foot bundle of energy, Wendy Campbell, who had come to Cornwall from milking her own herd of goats in Wiltshire, by way of a converted 60 ft MFV boat, last used in the War. Anchored in a creek in Gweek, Wendy soon needed an outlet for her energies and, happily for us, came up the hill to spend six fruitful years making 'Menallack Farmhouse'.

It was obvious, though, that her love still lay with goats so we gave her space and equipment to produce her own two cheeses using goat's milk with the help of her daughter.

Fingals and its brother cheese, initially called Cornish Feta but now changing to comply with labelling requirements, had an idyllic start. The milk was collected from a charming farm looking down on the upper reaches of the Fal and was taken across the historic King Harry Ferry to wind its way back through country lanes to Menallack. Fingals, using milk from just this one herd of Frieslands, is pasteurised and vegetarian renneted as are all of the Menallack cheeses. The curds are spooned into narrow tubes and left to drain for thirty hours. Fingals is either gently rolled in tarragon and lemon grass for a fresh alternative on the cheese board, or left simply plain.

Given the nature of goat curds, slow drainage gives a fresh cheese, which after brining can develop to quite a solidity. This firmness is much prized by chefs and private customers alike for its ability to be sliced and grilled, then placed on a bed of roasted peppers. Try it also coated with herbed breadcrumbs and gently baked on a purée of celeriac.

Cornish pepper is one of three fresh cheeses made from cows' milk at the Lynher Dairy, and which are among the freshest and simplest cheeses. All are made without rennet and flavoured individually. The cracked black pepper used for Cornish Pepper permeates right through the cheese, giving a tingle in the mouth from beginning to end.

Cornish Garlic and Herb is blended in and covered with a savoury mix of garlic and parsley; it has proved to be one of the most popular cheeses in Cornwall. Whether in a picnic or a simple lunch, an addition to a working day lunchbox or the soft part of a cheeseboard, Cornish Garlic and Herb is here to stay.

Cornish Tarragon is the third and most recent variation. Tarragon oil is introduced to the curds and the chopped leaf of the herb coats the outside.

Cousin Herbert is produced by Sue Proudfoot at Whalesborough Farm outside Bude. It is a delightful fresh lactic curd, sold in convenient little 113 g tubs. Who was Cousin Herbert? What was his importance in Sue's family that his memory is enshrined in chives and garlic or cracked pepper? This is another candidate for the picnic basket.

Nanterrow. Another cheesemaker in Cornwall when we arrived back was Dr Caroline Cheetham, who, with her husband Bob, had their own flock of sheep on an idyllic smallholding overlooking Carbis Bay.

Milking your own animals and then going on to make cheese is a more than full-time occupation, especially when there are young children mixed up in the equation. Caroline was at that time making not only the most delightful soft cheese, both plain and herbed, but also a hard cheese. When she and Bob decided a return to their previous careers was more sensible for a growing family, I persuaded my husband that this cheese could not just drop into oblivion. We brought it into Menallack and set about sourcing ewe's milk in Cornwall.

Nanterrow (for such was the name of their farm) continues to attract admirers wherever it goes – although, as I have said previously, fresh cheese and long journeys do not really mix.

It is a tangy cheese, either in a version with chives, parsley and garlic or the plain simplicity of the curds ladled straight into the mould, and is unbelievably delicious baked with fish, cubed and lightly folded into a salad or steamed summer vegetables. The plain Nanterrow, thinly sliced and fanned out on a pretty plate, is welcomed by our continental visitors for breakfast.

Buffalo Soft. A few years ago Menallack was approached by an enterprising young farmer just over the border in Devon. With the state of farming getting ever more gloomy, Mike Greenway had decided to think laterally and import a buffalo milking herd from Romania – and would we consider making a cheese from their milk? We automatically assumed we would be looking at a mozzarella style production, and did in fact try this for several weeks, but experience soon showed that a fresh cheese, demonstrating the cholesterol benefits of this milk, was far more appropriate to the south-west. Buffalo Soft is now a real winner with all those people fighting their doctors to get a little more cheese into their daily diet.

Mixed Fresh Cheeses
Heligan
Mrs Finn
Treverva

At Menallack, we take a leaf out of the continental cheese dairies and mix cow's and ewe's milk together with a little extra cream to make another group of soft cheeses. Some years ago, Tim Smit of The Lost Gardens of Heligan was delighted with the idea that the gardens should have not only their pineapples and other garden produce, but also a cheese.

Heligan uses these creamy blended milks, lightly covered with lemon shreds and decorated on the outside with the silver willow leaf of the gardens' name – for *heligenn* means 'willows'.

Mrs Finn commemorates the centenary of a charity originated by a redoubtable Victorian lady. This plain 4in round soon became celebrated as a thoroughly up-to-date fondue. Minimally heated and surrounded with the fresh young vegetables of the county, it makes a far more acceptable dip than the highly calorific classic alternative.

Treverva is named after the small village in which Menallack is to be found. Crushed green peppercorns have a fragrant sophistication not shared at all by the more robust black peppercorn. The little half-moon is coated with these peppercorns to permeate the *pâte* most appetisingly.

Making your own Cheese

Leaning over my stall in a market or show or talking to a group of ladies seated in a vestry on a wet blustery night at the end of Cornwall, I am continually asked two questions. 'Why did you start to make cheese?' – and quickly following on – 'Could I make some cheese in my own kitchen? Is it very difficult and complicated?' My answer is always geared to encouragement and 'have a go' optimism.

Any housewife who has spent a fair amount of her time raising and feeding a family will have walked her fingers through many recipes to find something new to please the faces round the table and – just as importantly – to prevent boredom from entering her daily cooking. The attention to detail, when reading those instructions next to an appetising picture, means that the housewife who would like to try her hand at making a cheese is already well on the road to success.

Making a cheese is yet one more recipe; and as with all food recipes the outcome will vary according the quality of the milk, the animal type, the ingredients and the method by which you choose to turn that gallon of milk into your very own milk solid.

Rather like breadmaking, making a cheese in your own kitchen has to be fitted into the rest of the day's routine. I made both in the farmhouse kitchen here and found that the necessary waiting periods for both were very compatible.

While the dough was rising under the stainless steel bowl covered with a towel, the milk could be gently ripening in that first stage of changing the fresh milk into curds and whey.

I was lucky in that I had inherited an Aga. This gave me the gentle background warmth for both jobs, but I am sure that the warmth can be achieved by many other ways, airing cupboards and sunny windows to think of only two.

As in breadmaking, any hurrying or speeding up of the process is fatal to the end product. For cheesemaking, any sudden increases of heat are also bad news for the delicate curd. Gently, gently is the secret, until experience tells you that the acidity of the curds has risen enough to set it on the next step, salting it and packing it into a muslin-lined mould.

Your first equipment can be chosen from what you already have around your kitchen – preserve pans, buckets, scales, thermometers, ham knives, cake tins or food tins (that have been scrupulously cleaned from their previous contents!) and fine draining cloths. (I was able to use some of the contents of my linen cupboard before starting to buy muslin specially for the purpose.)

One lady I spoke to in the very early days at Menallack had a ready supply of fresh cream. I made my envy plain at such a wonderful start to achieving some delicious dairy foods. But I just could not convince her that she would not need state of the art equipment before she could begin!

One of the simplest cheeses – cottage cheese – is one which we have all inadvertently made, by leaving our daily milk to sour in the container! This is perhaps the best cheese with which to start your career in the dairy. Pouring the curds into a draining sack of soft open material and leaving it suspended over a broomstick between chairs, and dripping into a tray below, will yield a very pleasant soft curd in one to three days which can then be scraped down from the cloth and carefully salted. Proceed with great caution at this stage as an over-salted soft cheese is most unattractive. Better to mix a very small amount of salt, taste, and then leave for a little while to allow the curd to take up the seasoning, as it will, and then deepen in flavour. Taste again, and consider whether a little chopped herb or spring onion might set the seal on your first try on the home dairy front.

There are some very good books, which any bookseller can order for you, about simple cheese making. Your library will also have an interesting group of books on this subject. Secondhand bookshops can also prove fruitful.

I can recommend a paperback entitled *Butter and Cheese*, by V Cheke and A Sheppard. Blotched and stained with whey, page 51 of my copy shows only too clearly how this page was kept open and close to hand during those early days. In effect a daily diary of my cheese making efforts and the results, it looks incredibly scruffy and dog eared; but it might comfort you if you are seeking for immaculate perfection coupled with dairy hygiene – a blotched record book is the happy indication to our regulatory authorities that you are taking day to day pains and not simply writing your results when you have washed up for the day!

Real excitement comes when producing a 'praper' little cheese that can sit on a board in a well ventilated cool room; with regular turning and handling of the rind over a month it will become what we call a 'householder cheese'.

Unlike the cottage cheese previously described, this cheese requires us to ripen it with a starter of carefully controlled bacteria, mix in a rennet to set the curd and after another period of time to cut the curd very carefully with a sharp knife so that the small cubes are not roughly handled and lose their vital contents into the surrounding whey.

These cubes of soft curd are then stirred gently with our hands for over forty minutes whilst the whey is very gently raised by $10°F$ ($6°F$) so that the cubes are scalded.

I found that I was able to raise this temperature most successfully in those early farm kitchen days by placing large lidded jars of either hot or cold water into the whey. I am sure that any direct contact with a more positive heat would have been far too fierce.

After forty minutes, the curds will have expelled some of the whey and, becoming heavier, will sink to the bottom of your vessel. At that stage we rest the curds, letting them mass together for fifteen minutes, and finally drain the whey off. Cutting the curds cleanly into handleable blocks allows more whey to drain off and the next step of making a cheese can then start.

This stage is known as 'working the curds'. By handling and breaking the curds in periods of once every fifteen minutes for about an hour and a half, we are driving the acidity of the curds up to the necessary level for making a firm cheese. There is a titration instrument to check this, but perfectly good cheese can be achieved by watching the state of the curd pieces as they continue to mature at this point.

When the curd has reached the stage at which it has a faintly acid taste and smell and is reasonably dry to the hand, it is broken into small walnut-sized pieces.

I used to ask my father to do this while he sat in the conservatory at the end of the kitchen. The dogs gathered round in case any pieces escaped from the bowl on his lap and fell to the floor! In the dairy, where there is fair amount of curd to be broken back into small pieces, one uses a hopper – not unlike a mincer, but far gentler in action. Salt is also added very carefully at this stage. Less is better than more; but just right is the best!

Very important at this stage, as with any young thing be it plants or babies, is to keep the dear thing warm. So we work fast, but gently, piling the curds into a mould lined with a hot, steeped and wrung-out muslin. With a gentle fist, we make sure that the curds are rammed well into the edges of the mould, using the smaller curds at the base and top of the mould to make a smooth surface, and pile the curds high above the rim before covering them tenderly with the top edges of the muslin.

On goes the lid or tray, or whatever you have to hand, to make quite sure that your young cheese is going to sit in its own warmth for an hour, whilst you make your cup of tea and relax to look over your work scene.

The end of the day is with us. The toddler cheese is now ready for bed. Between one and two hours after the curds have been shaped into the mould, we give them another 'topping and tailing', reversing their position in the mould and wrapping them in a refreshed warm muslin.

Now! – to find a simple place for them to rest, and something to keep them under pressure – for three days. Most of us have, lurking in dark cupboards, those heavy weights of a pound and more, so essential in pre-metric days and before scales had dials. They are real antiques, to be treasured. But other things will do just as well – even a lovely piece of granite – just choose one with a fairly level base!

During this very important pressing time, which can vary from as little as twelve hours right through to my suggested three days, I would advise a regular check on your baby. Refresh the muslin (or nappy, as I am quite happy to call the cloth!) and look at the surface of the cheese very carefully each time, making sure that it is matting well together on the first inspection and, before the end of the pressing period, make sure that the top follower (the disc fitting inside the mould) is lying evenly. No one wants a tilted baby!

You have tipped your baby out of his mould for the last time; you think nothing has ever looked quite so beautiful.

Round, smooth and golden and smelling quite delicious; but that baby has now got to grow up. The tricky path to maturity lies ahead with possible hazards on every side. How are you going to keep this young thing so that it can achieve all the promise that you have placed in it?

If it is left in your kitchen, where hopefully there is very little dampness around to turn your leathers mouldy and spot up your linens, your baby cheese will grow dryer and dryer. That wonderful smooth surface over which you took such pains will begin to crack open and all the natural spores floating around our domestic scene will happily invade those cracks and quickly cause real havoc in the inner curd – unless of course you are intending to make a blue cheese and even then I would not advise achieving it in quite such an undisciplined way!

Back to my linen cupboard for me, with a thank-you to my parents for passing on so much frail bed linen to me when they gave up the family home. I was able to tear up strips of old school sheets, still with name tape sewn on neatly at the bottom corner, and bandage my little cheese truckle, sewing a disc to the bandage at top and bottom.

I could have made a flour paste and anointed the surfaces with this, but I didn't. I could have rubbed some lard or butter all over the young thing, but I didn't. I could have bought some cheese wax, but I only did this in the following year. Boiling wax is like boiling oil for a medieval punishment!

However, I have to admit that I am blessed here at Menallack Farm with a number of deep, north- and east-facing window embrasures. These did me very well for the first year; and there was always the dairy across the yard!

So look around you, if you are going down the cheese-making trail, see what you can make use of in your own environment. Some of my customers have bought a young Menallack and matured it on in their cellar for a year! Others have been happy to use an old fashioned meat-safe in a cool garage.

The maturity of your cheese offspring is governed by its size. If you have been able to produce a whopper, then that whopper is going to take some time to achieve maturity – but a small wee thing (far more likely for most of us on the domestic front) is going to dry out quicker with the proportionally larger surface area of the rind. As drying out also checks the ripening action by which you want your truckle to turn into cheesey cheese, you have a fine deciding line at which your knife is itching to get at your baby and taste that home-made cheese; or, like Abraham, you stay the weapon and grant it grace to mature on for another spell. The decision is yours; but don't forget to make a note of it in that disgracefully dirty notebook of yours!

Where to buy Cornish Cheeses

Every year it becomes easier to buy Cornish cheeses and other local produce in shops and even supermarkets across the county and into Devon, and the enthusiastic retail outlets are now too numerous to list.

For those further afield, by far the easiest way to obtain Cornish cheese is to contact us here at Menallack. We have a welcoming farm shop here, but we also supply to both private and retail customers, by post or delivery.

Cornish Farmhouse Cheeses
Menallack Farm, Treverva, Penryn, Cornwall, TR10 9BP
Tel/fax (01326) 340333   e-mail: menallack@FSBdial.co.uk
www.Cornishfarmhousecheeses.com

Lynher Farms and Dairies, Netherton, Upton Cross, Liskeard, PL14 5BD welcome viewing and sell their own cheeses.
Tel: (01579) 362244 www.cornishyarg.co.uk

Whalesborough Farm Foods, Marhamchurch, Bude, EX23 0JD
Contact: Sue Proudfoot   (01288) 361317
e-mail: fraser.proudfoot@farmersweekly.net

The Cornish Cheese Company, Knowle Farm, Upton Cross, PL14 5BG   Contact: Philip Stanfield   (01579) 363660

Cornish Country Larder Ltd, The Creamery, Trevarrian, Newquay, TR8 4AH
Contact John Gaylard   (01637) 860331   www.ccl–ltd.co.uk